FANTASTIC

Three enchanting illus
to delight and ins

Stories by Robert Eshelby
Illustrated by Ruth Eshelby

Dedicated to Jenny Eshelby,
a great networker

THE MAGIC OF TWO

The Numbers Game

Story by Robert Eshelby
Illustrated by Ruth Eshelby

Many, many years ago, somewhere in the north-west of what was then India and is now Pakistan, and not very far from the ancient Kingdom of Persia, now called Iran, a man sat under an awning in the middle of a market place, drinking tea. As he watched the townsfolk pass him busily by, the man was joined by a distinguished-looking stranger. He, too, ordered a cup of tea from the tea-seller and spoke.

"Nice day," he offered.

The other man turned slowly towards the stranger, "Is it? I cannot say. My dream has turned sour and the world means nothing to me any more."

Following such a response, most of us would have hastened to take our cup of tea elsewhere. However, the stranger was curious and did not shy away.

"Tell me your name, if you please, sir, and tell me about this dream which you have lost."

"Very well, but you must not interrupt me. My name is Sissa. As you can see, I am a Brahmin by birth, a man of privilege and education. I have spent all my adult years creating a wonderful game, a game of life and death, of warfare and power; a game so wonderful that it has taken over my soul.

"All my inheritance has been wasted on manufactuing wooden boards and carving beautiful ivory armies for this game.

"I have a team of the finest craftsmen assisting me. With their help, I have dreamed of sharing my new game of life with the civilised world. In doing so, I had hoped to restore my family's fame and fortune. Alas, I did not realise how hard it would be to sell my game.

"I have given many sets away to my friends, in the hope of inspiring their interest in this game, but no-one wants to play, let alone buy a set. I am sure that there must be people of intelligence, who would value a game which trains them to think ahead, to plan, to be resourceful and, ultimately, to triumph over adversity. Alas! I have more than a thousand sets sitting in my warehouse and my workers sit idle. My wife won't speak to me. My dream has become my despair."

"My dear fellow," replied the stranger, "You are in a predicament. You have your dream, but no-one will share this dream with you and restore your fortunes. Why not show me your game and I will see if I can help."

Sissa's face lifted a little as he reached into a blue cotton bag he wore strapped across his shoulders. He pulled out an ornate black and white chequered board of about a foot square and laid it lovingly on the table. Then, with great care, he set out his ivory pieces, in order, on the board.

"I call my game 'chess', which in ancient times meant 'check'. A player is a powerful king with a great army. The idea is that your army checks the advance of your opponent. After a mighty battle, the winner is the player who makes the best tactical moves and, thus, defeats the other's army. Let me show you what I mean."

The pieces looked like two great armies, one made of white ivory, the other stained red. They were intricately and lovingly carved. Each a masterpiece of the craftsman's art. The stranger took in the beauty set before him. There were kings and queens, foot soldiers and knights. There were elephants from India with jewelled tusks, and trunks joyfully uplifted. There were castles of such magnificence that the stranger could only wonder at them. "Are they not amazing? Do you not feel the blood coursing through your veins just to look at them?"

They set to work with a will; the one army led by Sissa, the dreamer, the other led by his King, for the stranger was indeed a great monarch, a man much taken to wandering his small kingdom unrecognized, worrying about the grinding poverty of most of his people, and watching carefully for any hint of unrest or revolution.

Finally, Sissa was defeated. The King was entranced. Here was a way of fighting wars without bloodshed, of entertaining his guests and keeping his subjects amused, when they might otherwise have plotted against him.

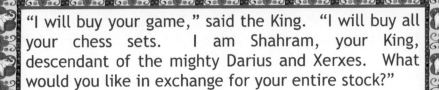

"I will buy your game," said the King. "I will buy all your chess sets. I am Shahram, your King, descendant of the mighty Darius and Xerxes. What would you like in exchange for your entire stock?"

Sissa, of course, collapsed to the floor in obeisance to this powerful King. At this point, his fortune would have been made, his future secure. Unfortunately, a cunning look had come over his face, the sort of foolish cunning which often spells disaster to its owner.

"My King, I do not ask much for this wonderful game, even though, as you have seen, it has taken years to invent and has the power to make its owner a fortune."

The King sighed, aware that he was now subject to a hard sell. "Yes, yes. Well, get on with it!"

"I do not seek gold. If you would just place one grain of wheat on the first square of my chess board and then double it, so that you place two grains on the second square, four on the third and so on, until every square is full, I'd happily be paid in wheat."

The King smiled at Sissa. "A most reasonable request and one which I shall grant. Allow me one moment, while I calculate how much I owe you."

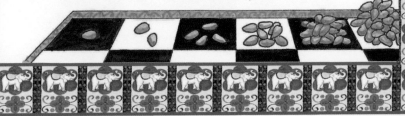

Now, there are sixty-four squares on a modern chess board, and goodness knows how many there were originally. With the tip of his tongue protruding between his lips and his pencil flying, King Shahram reached the twenty-first square before he looked up. He gazed at Sissa with no hint of kindness—gone was the sense of benevolence and understanding which had previously been between the two men. This was very definitely a King talking to his erring subject.

"On the twenty first square, I calculate that I will already have paid you 1,048,576 grains of wheat. I estimate that, by the time I complete the board, I will owe you more than 18 million, million, million grains of wheat. I have never counted the number of grains of wheat in a sack, but without doubt, your game of life will have bankrupted my kingdom and left all my subjects to starve. You, on the other hand, would be richer than any Nabob in India. What do you have to say for yourself?"

Sissa was a clever man, who had not expected his King to be quite so smart. Also, the chess board squares and the wheat grains had been the product of an inspired moment. He hadn't really had time to work through his own calculation. Being clever, Sissa held his tongue and quietly squirmed and grovelled before his King. What came next underlined the level of what had become a great miscalculation.

"Nothing to say? Well, perhaps it is wiser, at this point, to leave it to me. I am a man of honour." said the King. "I keep my word, especially when it's given in public." He smiled.

"Fortunately for me, but less fortunately for you, our deal was made in private, so I do not feel so badly about going against my word. You struck a bad bargain with me. Now I shall strike off your head! Tomorrow morning, here in the market-place, you shall be rewarded for your greed at the hands of the public executioner. But first, you shall spend the night in your cell counting the number of grains of wheat in a sack. Take him away!"

The plain-clothed body-guards led Sissa off to the dungeon to await his punishment and to spend a sleepless night counting innumerable grains of wheat.

The King, meanwhile, slung Sissa's bright blue bag over his shoulder and walked back to his palace with a jaunty step.

King Shahram pondered all night as he practised chess, alone. He thought of his poverty and of the magical way the grains of wheat had grown from one to one million in such a short time. He thought very hard indeed.

The next day, on the very spot where Sissa had so outraged him, King Shahram waited until the executioner's axe was raised. Just as it was about to fall on Sissa's neck, the King roared, "Stop!" This was fortunate for Sissa, who could not believe he had gone from bankrupted to beheaded in such a short space of time, and was contemplating how life can always get worse, even when you think you are in the worst position possible.

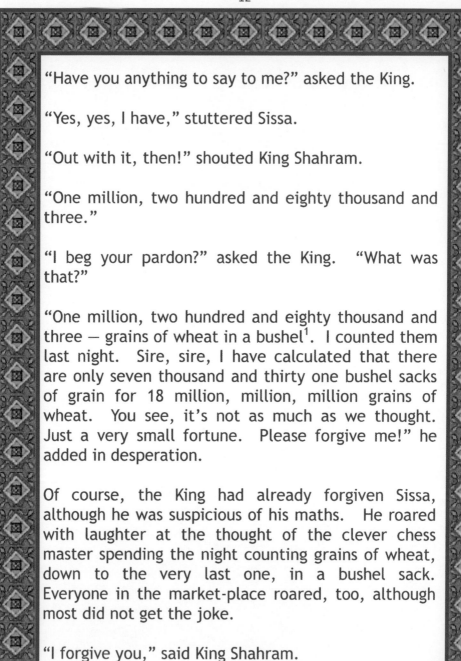

"Have you anything to say to me?" asked the King.

"Yes, yes, I have," stuttered Sissa.

"Out with it, then!" shouted King Shahram.

"One million, two hundred and eighty thousand and three."

"I beg your pardon?" asked the King. "What was that?"

"One million, two hundred and eighty thousand and three — grains of wheat in a bushel[1]. I counted them last night. Sire, sire, I have calculated that there are only seven thousand and thirty one bushel sacks of grain for 18 million, million, million grains of wheat. You see, it's not as much as we thought. Just a very small fortune. Please forgive me!" he added in desperation.

Of course, the King had already forgiven Sissa, although he was suspicious of his maths. He roared with laughter at the thought of the clever chess master spending the night counting grains of wheat, down to the very last one, in a bushel sack. Everyone in the market-place roared, too, although most did not get the joke.

"I forgive you," said King Shahram.

[1] A bushel was equal to 64 lbs or 29 kilos

"May I remove my head from the block now, my lord," enquired Sissa, "before the headsman does so on my behalf?" One felt that he, too, was warming to the joke.

"Yes, yes, get up! Please get up and come here," replied his King. "Thank you very much, headsman, you may go. Oh, but first," he held up his hand to prevent the executioner from leaving, "Sissa, will you agree to sell me all your one thousand chess sets and the right to manufacture and market all the sets in the future? I will pay you ten rupees for each set and ten thousand rupees for the business, making you the sum of twenty thousand rupees. As part of the deal, I want you to play chess with me in the market-place every day for one week."

Sissa could not believe his ears. His life had been spared and he had been made rich. All his dreams would be fulfilled. He nodded his head vigorously, very relieved that it was still attached to his body. Twenty thousand rupees! (At this point, it would be wise to remember that the modern rupee does not buy as much as it used to.)

"Let us sit down and play chess and immediately start to improve the fortunes of our poor nation. I have thought hard about the way a grain of wheat doubles from one to thousands at such speed. This principle, which I have named 'The Magic of Two', will make our Kingdom rich, and all because of your game of chess." The King took out the board and set up the game. "By the way, tell your men to start work again. I want ten thousand chess sets ready for when your thousand have been distributed."

Sissa gulped and then concentrated on losing the game of chess, lest once again he should be in danger of losing his head.

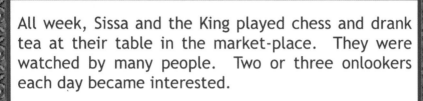

All week, Sissa and the King played chess and drank tea at their table in the market-place. They were watched by many people. Two or three onlookers each day became interested.

At the end of the week, the King shook Sissa by the hand, "That is all. Thank you for your help." The two parted. Sissa went home to his smiling wife, Parvin, with his twenty thousand rupees. The King took two men on one side and talked earnestly with them over a cup of tea. "I don't know what he is up to," mused Sissa, "But I would stake my fortune that it won't sell chess sets."

Although only a few chess sets were sold from the palace shop over the next week or two, the demand slowly increased. The chess craftsmen were working at full speed for the King, and turning out hundreds of sets each week. Suddenly, after ten weeks, the warehouse was stripped of its original one thousand sets. In six months, the workers couldn't keep up with their orders. Craftsmen came from far and near to help.

One day, Sissa was sitting in the market-place, drinking his cup of tea, when a squadron of horsemen came by, led by King Shahram, dressed in magnificent armour. Seeing the chessmaster, King Shahram dismounted and ordered a cup of tea.

"You're looking prosperous," said the King.

"Thanks to you, I'm very comfortable. I wish I had your money, though. I should have kept the game to myself."

"Yes, it was certainly your game. It was your grains of wheat that gave me the germ of my idea of the Magic of Two. Mind you, if you had been left to your own devices, you would be completely ruined and your game would still be gathering dust."

"The last time I saw you," said Sissa, "I wouldn't have given you any chance of selling my game. What did you do?"

"I thought hard first. I needed to introduce it to as many people as possible. Above all, I needed to find the right people to market my game. The Magic of Two is so great that I only had to find two people who were as passionate as I was about the game. They had to buy one set each for their own pleasure. Then I helped them to find two people in exactly the same way as I had. In other words, I wanted to duplicate my idea. All they had to do was to sit in their village market place and play chess, just as we did, then sell a set each to two enthusiasts and help these customers to do the same. However, there were a few vital ingredients which everyone needed to use if the system was to work."

"A smooth tongue," suggested Sissa.

"You have a smooth tongue and look where you nearly ended up!" the King replied.

"A slogan?.... I don't know," he gave up.

"Well, they all seem to start with the letter 'C'. Every member of the team had to emphasise these C's. It wasn't enough for them to **Care** passionately about chess. They had to be available to help the two people they were sponsoring. They had to make a **Commitment** to the success of everyone's business because their own success depended upon it. They had to choose their customers carefully and to realise that there would be problems to solve. As for **Courage**, well, it takes courage to hold on to your dream, to sponsor two people, help them in their own sponsoring and trust in them. With the right people, the right system and the right attitude in place, there should be no need for more.

"So I sat back and waited. Within ten generations of my plan, we had sold a thousand sets, but only because everyone involved was equally committed. I made myself available at the palace shop, in case I could help things along. As expected, another ten generations took us up to one million sales. Now everyone has heard of chess, from Calcutta to Teheran. I have built up my army and my empire, so I can play the game of life like a real King. I still play chess in the evenings, though, as it keeps my brain in good order."

Sissa's mind reeled at the simplicity of the King's marketing stratagem.

"Now that I have shown you how to market an idea, starting with just two people, I wonder if you've invented another game, which might provoke some interest among my subjects?"

"Well, my lord," said Sissa thoughtfully, "I have been working on something. I thought it might do for the person who *doesn't* like chess."

"Go on," encouraged the King.

"Have you ever thought of pitting two armies together in a mock battle? You give them an inflated sheep's bladder to kick. The winning team is the one which kicks the sheep's bladder between two trees the most often in a day. Or you could make it

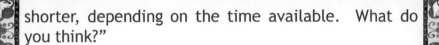

shorter, depending on the time available. What do you think?"

The King looked scornfully at him. "What will you call it? Sheepsbladder? I don't think so. It sounds like a dud to me."

They shook hands and the King went on his way.

If Sissa had been riding alongside the King, he would have been amazed at the way the King was muttering and laughing to himself. He would have been seriously upset, however, if he could have known what it was that the King was saying: "'Bladderball, a game played by two armies. A game for those who prefer real action to a chessboard.' I like it! Now I wonder if I can find a thousand sheep's bladders..."

He rode on, singing a song he had composed himself.

"How do you make your dreams come true?

♪   Abracadabra!   ♪

The Magic of Two!"

Footnote:

The game of 'Bladderball' was first played in the north-west of India in the sixth century AD.

A variation was played with severed heads in Mongolia at the time of Kubla Khan.

The game was popular among soldiers in the British colonial army.

It was re-christened 'football' in the nineteenth century and has even reached the far Americas in the early 21st century.

Football, or soccer, is still played today, especially by people who find chess insufficiently stimulating.

The End

Maybe,
a new beginning...

A Corncrake

Finding Your Voice

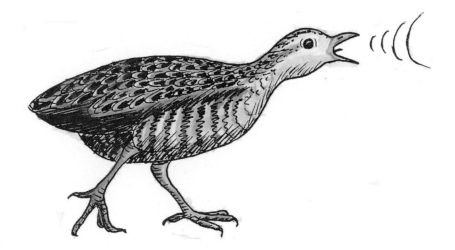

Story by Robert Eshelby
Illustrated by Ruth Eshelby

One morning, some time after the last light in the street had been turned off and well before the light of dawn, Jimmy's father was heard by his wife to mutter, "OK, OK, I'll get him or he'll wake the neighbourhood up."

Jimmy did, in fact, wake the neighbours up, frequently.

When he cried, his body would puff up like a bullfrog. His face would contract with effort and his mouth, all gums and tongue, would open up like a letter box. The sound that burst forth was somewhere between the shriek of a car alarm and the incredibly debilitating sound encountered by an intruder in Mr. Jessop's well-alarmed, home-is-his-castle semi-detached next door.

Jimmy's parents didn't need a burglar alarm.

Jimmy's parents didn't need
a burglar alarm.

is mother was worried. What could be the problem with Jimmy? What could possibly hurt that much? Was he always hungry? Did he have a blockage in his bowel?

There had to be a reason for the rumpus every night. Was he just sensitive? Jimmy's father suggested that the boy was obviously a bad lot from the start, and probably got it from his mother's side. This did not relieve the tension, although Jimmy's father was obviously amused at the thought.

Some children perform rocking movements to help them sleep. Others can be heard talking delightful nonsense before succumbing to Morpheus. Jimmy, on the other hand, in a manner more brutal than musical, chose to serenade the neighbours with a series of vocal gymnastics worthy of the Valkyries at full gallop. Suddenly, without warning, sleep would fall on Jimmy, just when everyone had started to wonder if the entertainment would ever stop. Anxious neighbours would find him asleep. Smiling and sighing contentedly to himself, he looked just like an angel.

He was lovely when awake, too; bright-eyed and obviously bright in other ways. He learned to talk at about eighteen months of age. At about that time, too, his parents' sleepless nights became fewer and fewer, until there was no more midnight howling. His mother began to get her colour back and lose the bags under her eyes. She could look the neighbours in the eye again. Jimmy's father was promoted and regained his old sense of humour. In short, the house became more relaxed and everyone in the street could breathe again.

Jimmy loved to sing. His mother sang nursery rhymes to him and his father taught him rugby songs with blanks where some of the words should have been. Jimmy used to join in 'Baa Baa Black Sheep' and 'Mademoiselle from Armentières' with equal gusto. His voice, however, left something to be desired. For a start, it was very loud, but it was also rough at the edges. His mother said he sounded like a corncrake. His father asked him if he could sing 'Far, Far Away', a joke which Jimmy did not get for years.

ne day, he plucked up courage and asked his mother what a corncrake was. With a sense of humour reminiscent of his father's, he asked, "Do you have it for breakfast with milk and sugar?" His mother ignored the pun and told him a corncrake was a shy bird, seldom to be seen and very rare these days. "The only way you know it's there is by its voice, which is loud and raucous. But never mind, dear – I'm sure the song of the corncrake sounds beautiful to his mother." Jimmy was little the wiser, and got to wondering if singing 'Far, Far Away' made any more sense. He also wondered if a corncrake could ever sing like a thrush, or would it even want to. And if it did, would its mother still love it?

hen little Jimmy sang, he would puff up like a bullfrog, his face would be contorted and his mouth would open as wide as a letterbox. It was just like when he was a baby – only with teeth. He loved this singing. When he was sixteen, he told his parents he wanted to be an opera singer. They laughed. "You can't sing," his father said, "We've heard you. You should become an accountant, like me." His mother smiled indulgently at him, "It would help if you had a voice," she said. "Your singing is like the sound of a rookery at dusk." Just as Jimmy was about to put in his oar, she continued, "But if you really want to sing, you can have lessons with Miss Sweet on the corner. Perhaps she can put you on the right track."

Well, she did. So much so that within a year or two, Jimmy's voice sounded quite normal. He listened to recordings of Caruso and Pavarotti and felt that, with hard work, he, too, could be a singer. Miss Sweet was always reminding him not to shout to tone down his voice so that it would blend. His voice was a tall poppy in the field of music. Blending was to become of paramount importance.

hen he was eighteen, Jimmy's voice had improved to such an extent that he was entered for an audition to study at a famous London college of music. At his audition, Jimmy sang 'Una Furtiva Lagrima', not like Caruso, but musically and with such a diminuendo that you could have heard a hairpin drop.

The Professor and three teachers listening to Jimmy had already heard several tenors that day who were all musical and whose singing was very tasteful, but none of it real singing. When Jimmy had finished his singing, the Professor said, rudely, "Yes, yes! But can you <u>sing</u>? Sing me something, anything, loudly and passionately. I want to hear your real voice!"

Jimmy's temper flared as he stalked back to the piano and started again. He was really angry and decided that he, too, could be rude. The only thing he could think of was 'Mademoiselle from Armentières' and he sang it with gusto, including the missing words. He sang like a bullfrog, his face contorted and his mouth wider than a letter box.

"That's done it!" he thought, when he'd finished. You certainly could not have heard a pin drop as Jimmy sang, but you certainly could have when he finished. The panel smiled at each other.

"That's more like it," said the Professor. "Poor choice of piece and voice like a corncrake, but we can do something with that."

ventually, he could sing in front of people who didn't know anything about singing, but knew what they liked – and they knew that they liked his voice.

Jimmy's parents were very proud of him when they heard him sing at the Albert Hall. "I told you so," said his father. "I always said he had a voice that could fill the Albert Hall. Mind you, I still think he should have been an accountant!"

If there is a moral to this tale, it should be:

Look for
your own voice
- we've all got one –
and never
let the doubters
spoil your dream.

But beware...

t might also be that you can train an ambitious corncrake for four years to become an opera singer and all you'll have is a well-trained corncrake.

It really doesn't matter. Either way they'll be happy.

Alternative ending:

> After four years of vocal training,
> Jimmy accepted the inevitable
> and became an accountant,
> and that was all right, too.

Points to Ponder

We are all unique.
Every one of us has something really
precious to offer.

- In what ways are we unique?
- How do we recognise our talent?
- What should we do with our talent?
- What if others can't see it?
- Should we listen to advice?
- What is success?
- What is failure?
- Should apparent failure put us off trying?
- At what point do we give up our dreams?
- How can we help our own children?
- Can hard work conquer all obstacles?
- Is it ever too late?

The Spider

Story by Robert Eshelby

Illustrated by Ruth Eshelby

It was a clear morning. The sun reflected off the fine frost which covered the ground. It was February on the allotments. The lavish vegetable growth of last summer was just a memory. Instead, the rectangular plots were bare, not even turned over yet for Spring. Only a few shrivelled onion heads were visible, or maybe a cabbage or two, run to seed. Otherwise all was just waiting for the frost to yield and for the busy growing cycle to start anew.

"Time for a chat," mused Young Bill, as he walked from his humble garden shed to Clarence House. "Time to hear what old Clarence is up to."

Long known as 'Clarence House' and with a hand-painted sign to support the fact, the house of Clarence, or (more accurately) the shed of Clarence was something wondrous.

At some point in Norman English history, there was a Duke of Clarence who is reported to have drowned in a butt (or barrel) of Malmsey wine. There is also a very grand house in the more fashionable part of London, which is called 'Clarence House' and was for many years the home of the late Queen Elizabeth, the Queen Mother. I need not tell you that Clarence was in no way related to either the Duke or the Queen Mother, but there was something superior about his allotment shed.

Some people can live their allotment days in a lean-to with nothing more than a table and chair, surrounded by seed packets, spades and rakes, trowels and scythes. When you came to Clarence House, you came to a palace among sheds, a debating chamber, an upper house of parliament of the shed world. Table, chairs, seeds, scythes, spades – yes, of course! But in this twelve by ten foot council chamber there was an old Turkish rug of some pretension on the hard, dirt floor. There was an Edwardian sideboard, too big for home but far too good to throw away. There was even a kitchen sink with a cold water tap fed by a green hosepipe, which snaked away over the floor and through a hole in the wall. On the wall, above the sideboard, was a picture of the Queen Mother, a whimsical reference to that other stately home.

"Come in!" boomed a voice from within, as Young Bill knocked. "What can I do for you? Not on the scrounge again, I trust?"

Young Bill, aged seventy-two next birthday, smiled at the repartee. He never scrounged, it was just one of Clarence's little jokes.

"Rosie Lee?" Clarence asked, putting the electric kettle on. "Gypsy Rose Lee, fortune-telling, tea leaves. D'you see? Cockney rhyming slang; Rosie Lee – cup of tea." Young Bill did know. The offer of a nice cup of tea was always accompanied by this little ritual.

Clarence was, you see, a man of great and indeterminate age, a profound thinker, a quipper of quips, a quoter of quotes, and a fount of jokes, jibes and profundities.

"Tea would be good, thank you, Clarence - no sugar, of course. It might cheer me up. I'm still feeling a bit down about my vegetables. I've lost confidence after... you know... last year. You may remember all my work and I won nothing at the Dorchester Show."

"Your marrows were good. Like tree trunks. You should have won the marrows."

"Second in the marrows. I couldn't get over that."

"Your leeks were like telegraph poles, and that monster cauliflower would have made cauliflower cheese for the whole Dorchester Town Football Club!"

"**E**xcept for the greenfly. I should have spotted that."

"True. Except for the greenfly."

"You see, I did great, as you might say. I couldn't have done better, but I still only got a commendation for my leeks and a disqualification because of the greenfly. I didn't win a thing."

"That reminds me of a story," said Clarence, as he poured tea into two cups of willow-pattern with matching saucers, and reached for the packet of Rich Tea biscuits. "Have you got a moment?"

"Cheers!" said Young Bill, as he picked up his tea and waited.

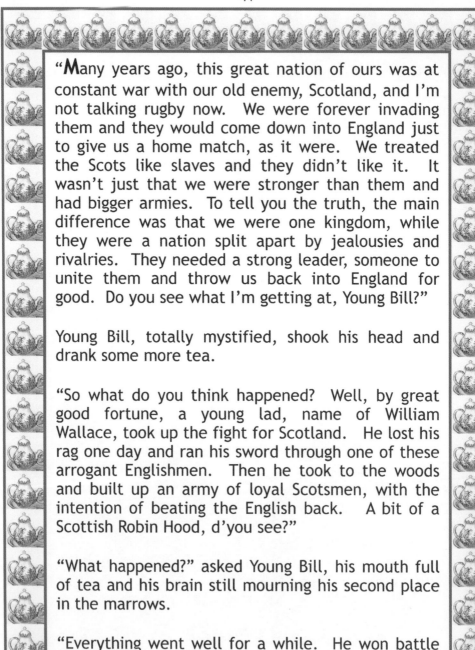

"**M**any years ago, this great nation of ours was at constant war with our old enemy, Scotland, and I'm not talking rugby now. We were forever invading them and they would come down into England just to give us a home match, as it were. We treated the Scots like slaves and they didn't like it. It wasn't just that we were stronger than them and had bigger armies. To tell you the truth, the main difference was that we were one kingdom, while they were a nation split apart by jealousies and rivalries. They needed a strong leader, someone to unite them and throw us back into England for good. Do you see what I'm getting at, Young Bill?"

Young Bill, totally mystified, shook his head and drank some more tea.

"So what do you think happened? Well, by great good fortune, a young lad, name of William Wallace, took up the fight for Scotland. He lost his rag one day and ran his sword through one of these arrogant Englishmen. Then he took to the woods and built up an army of loyal Scotsmen, with the intention of beating the English back. A bit of a Scottish Robin Hood, d'you see?"

"What happened?" asked Young Bill, his mouth full of tea and his brain still mourning his second place in the marrows.

"Everything went well for a while. He won battle after battle, but unfortunately he was betrayed and executed in a most unpleasant way by the English."

"That's not a very uplifting story," said Young Bill. "He failed, didn't he?"

"Why, yes, in the end, but he was a real hero and never gave up. It takes guts to keep going when you're fighting a losing battle. Now who was it had to try, try and try again, before he succeeded?"

Young Bill gleefully picked up the reference, scarcely able to contain himself. "Robert the Bruce! Don't tell me! He was in exile watching this spider climb up its web. It kept falling down and starting again. When it finally succeeded in climbing up the thread, it inspired him to beat the English:

> 'At Bannockburn in 1314
> The English fought the Scots, unsporting.'

I learnt that the Scots dug pits, filled them with pointed sticks and covered them with turf. When the English cavalry attacked, they fell into the pits and were seriously impaled!"

Clarence smiled, his eyes glinting behind his steel-rimmed glasses. "Very good. Like everyone else, you remember all the wrong things you learnt at primary school.

"You know, ostriches don't bury their heads in sand and carrots don't help you to see in the dark. It's all rumour; rumour and speculation. No, no, Robert the Bruce didn't watch spiders, at least, not out of curiosity. That's the whole point – he hated spiders. He didn't know it at the time, but he was an arachnophobe. He wouldn't go near them after his well-meaning grandmother told him to sleep with his mouth closed or he would breathe in spiders while he slept. It kept him awake for weeks. Another of your myths, of course, but he wasn't to know that.

"Look, when Robert the Bruce was defeated by the English and fled to the Western Isles of Scotland, the last place he wanted to live was in a cave. He just didn't have any choice. He was a well-bred young chap. He was petrified of the dark. He didn't like sleeping on bracken in case there were creepy crawlies in it. He was terrified of mice and was known to utter a very high-pitched scream if he ever saw a snake, of which, I may say, there are thousands in the Western Isles of Scotland. And then, there were the spiders."

"But I thought Robert the Bruce was a real warrior," said Young Bill, his face full of puzzlement.

"So he was. Just listen! Robert had no choice but to live in that dark, rodent-infested cave, together with his most trusted men. He was more terrified of the dark, the spiders, the creepy crawlies, the mice and the snakes than he was of the English. One night, he lay on the bed of bracken, trying to go to sleep, with his candle lit, as usual, when he saw the spider trying to climb up its thread to the roof above where he was lying.

"Every time the spider fell back, it plummeted towards him, and he would shriek and wake up his soldiers. By the time this had happened three times, the soldiers picked him up and threw him out of the cave."

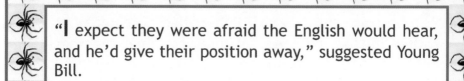

"I expect they were afraid the English would hear, and he'd give their position away," suggested Young Bill.

"Not a bit of it," said Clarence. "They just didn't want to lose their beauty sleep. Anyway, he hot-footed down the hill to the house of an old lady, who was known to be very wise and also very rich. He knocked on her door and asked for a bed for the night. As you might imagine, she wasn't keen, especially when he tried to tell her that he was the rightful King of Scotland. 'A likely story!' she would have thought, but she offered him a bed in the stable, out of the kindness of her heart. 'That'll be ten shillings,' she told him. Of course, Robert couldn't possibly sleep in the stable. It was dark and full of rats, mice and spiders. When Robert told her that he'd just been kicked out of the cave for such problems, the rich, wise lady beckoned him into her brightly lit, warm parlour. 'Give me a pound,' she said, 'and I'll help you to get rid of all this nonsense. Tell me about all these fears of yours.'

"Robert explained about his granny, the snakes, the rats, the mice, the fear of the dark and, last of all, the spiders. The old lady sat for a while, her head reeling, her hand clutching tightly the golden sovereign he had given her. Finally, in her native Gallic, she gave him her verdict. He seemed to be fearful of everything small. This indicated to her that he was afraid of failure in large matters.

"'You suffer from complex phobias, which you can only overcome by a process of desensitisation. In other words, you will have to confront your fears if you are ever to overcome them.' These may not have been her exact words," said Clarence, "but you get my drift."

"But what about 'Try, try and try again'?" asked Young Bill. "That must come into it somewhere."

"Why, of course it does," replied Clarence, "I was just coming to that. The old lady, in her wisdom, had just finished her post-Freudian analysis of Robert. She still clutched the gold coin in her hand and thought fast on her feet. 'What I want you to do, is to go back to your cave right now. Lie in your bed every night for a week and think nice thoughts about spiders until you lose your fear of them. If you panic you must go back to your bed and try, try, try again.'" Clarence looked knowingly at Young Bill. "'Finally, you will be freed of your fear of spiders and might even want to keep one in a

matchbox as a pet. When you are ready, come back to me and we will deal with the rodents, the dark and the serpents. Phobias cost a sovereign each. Cheap, don't you think?'"

"Did he do it?" asked Young Bill.

"What, fall for the old lady's trap? Of course he did. It cost him five pounds to be rid of his phobias. Therapy wasn't cheap, even in those days."

"No, I meant, did he beat the English and become head of an independent Scotland?"

"Why, certainly he did. He confronted all his doubts and fears, until he had nothing else to fear. At that point, he put his spider in his matchbox and headed for Bannockburn – and even you know what happened at that battle. (Mind you, I take issue with you about the pointed sticks being unsporting, but that's another matter.) You see, once you've conquered your inner fears, you can easily face the big things in life, like 'What is my destiny? How am I going to pay the bills? How can I defeat the English?...'"

"...Am I going to win first prize for my leeks at next year's Dorchester Show?" interrupted Young Bill.

"Exactly! They become more achievable. If every-one in Scotland had done what Robert did, they'd have conquered the world, let alone the English."

"Look," said young Bill, "I enjoyed your story, but I'm not sure it sorts out my problems. I wanted advice, not a story. I still feel like giving up my allotment."

"**D**idn't my story teach you anything?" asked Clarence. "Who sorted Robert the Bruce out?"

"Why, the old lady."

"No! She made five pounds for a few sensible suggestions. In the end, it was all up to him. My suggestion to you is to forget about last year's marrows. There's nothing shameful in failure. You just keep trying until you succeed, or go down fighting. Try picturing your marrows with a blue rosette and you're halfway there. If you want something badly enough, try, try, try again. If at first you don't succeed, what do you do?"

"Give up?" said Young Bill, smiling.

"I can't see you giving up," said Clarence. "You've been winning prizes for twenty years. That'll be a pound."

Young Bill looked at him in surprise.

"Just kidding! Biscuit?"

Postscript

"Was there anything else about Robert the Bruce?" asked Young Bill.

"Well, he is credited with inventing the well-known cowboy trick of putting his horses' shoes on back-to-front so that his pursuers would think he was fast approaching them, when he was, in fact, running away from them; or indeed, think that he was running away from them when he was fast approaching them. This ploy would, of course, only work if your pursuers were some way behind you and out of sight, or they would only have to look at the horse to see which direction it was really travelling in," explained Clarence.

"And," said Young Bill, "if you were following him and the horse's shoes were on back to front, he would either just have passed you going the other way, in which case you would have seen him and caught him, or you would turn round and follow the direction of the horse shoes back to where he'd just been."

"Exactly. Clever, wasn't he? More tea?"

The End
Time for Change ?

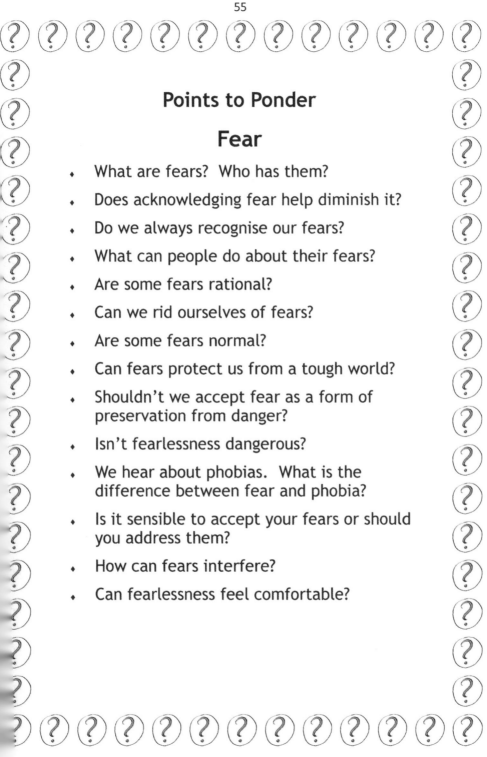

Points to Ponder

Fear

- What are fears? Who has them?
- Does acknowledging fear help diminish it?
- Do we always recognise our fears?
- What can people do about their fears?
- Are some fears rational?
- Can we rid ourselves of fears?
- Are some fears normal?
- Can fears protect us from a tough world?
- Shouldn't we accept fear as a form of preservation from danger?
- Isn't fearlessness dangerous?
- We hear about phobias. What is the difference between fear and phobia?
- Is it sensible to accept your fears or should you address them?
- How can fears interfere?
- Can fearlessness feel comfortable?

Further Discussion...

The Power of One

There is a tide in the affairs of men,
Which, taken at the flood, leads one on to fortune.
Shakespeare (Julius Caesar)

King Ethelred the Unready was the son of a great king and the grandson of a greater king. When his moment of glory came, he ruined the budding English nation. He failed to prevent the Viking Invasion, despite paying ruinous bribes, and turned years of peace and stability into warfare and bloodshed.

Other people, like Churchill, Ghandi, Kennedy and Mandela, rise to the occasion and become great leaders. They have a charisma, which allows them to lead other people, to influence them and to inspire them. Even if you don't agree with everything they do, you would still call them great. Take away their trappings of rank and wealth and they would still be great people.

What is their secret?
Surely we can't all aspire to greatness?

It is all a question of scale. If we change the concept of Greatness to that of Leadership, then understanding what constitutes leadership is of real value to us all.

We are all potential leaders.

Here are the key qualities of a leader:

- **Integrity and honesty of purpose**
- **A sense of mission or vision**
- **Decision-making** In an emergency, being decisive and wrong is usually better than making no decision.
- **Knowledge** The best decisions are made on the basis of knowledge.
- **Courage** Great leaders overcome their fears. Fear undermines success.
- **Self-confidence** This is attained only when all the other qualities have been achieved. Leaders inspire confidence in others.

'Cometh the hour, cometh the man'

Even if the big moment never comes and we are never to be players on the world's stage, working on these attributes will help us in our daily lives and at work.

We can all be leaders in our community, at work and in our business and family lives. We can strive to empower ourselves and to make a difference.

Once we have identified our shortcomings and overcome our fears, especially the fear of success, we will be ready to step on to our surfboards and ride the wave to fortune!

Printed in Poland
by Amazon Fulfillment
Poland Sp. z o.o., Wrocław

21060675R00036